STOP

WE MUST

STOP

USING MORE THAN OUR SHARE!

Humans are requiring one and a half Earths to support us!

Our carbon economy no longer fits our planet.

We must STOP hoping it's not as devastating as it is.

TURN!

We must TURN
and <u>can</u> TURN…
To Earth-size ways!
Meaning …
full empowerment of women!
zero waste cities!
low-meat diets!
wellbeing, instead of craving more!
love and wonder!

MERGE

**Because we can't do it alone.
But together we can fulfill our
desire for Earth-size living.
We can hone practices so
compelling that supersize,
MultiEarth ways become obsolete!**

FORM!

or JOIN!

A JUBILEE CIRCLE

Here's your
handbook on how.
Ready? Let's go.

First, What Is A Jubilee Circle?

Circles are groups of 2-6 persons who meet at least once per month in order to hone our personal and collective pursuits of OneEarth living.

As **Participants,** we continually seek to understand more fully the supersize, MultiEarth forces against which we struggle. These forces are wily. We continually seek to cleanse ourselves of their influence and displace the MultiEarth ways of death with OneEarth ways that bring life. All participants live with the consciousness that

Jubilee doesn't work well when we try going it alone. It's radically communitarian and democratic.

Circles are think tanks and animation cells. They are not committees. In these energy cells, we ignite one another's imaginations and empower each other's calls to action. We measure our individual and collective actions with the questions: Does it fit the planet? Is it good for all beings?

Circles benefit from a continuous 3-part cycle of action, reflection, and analysis. It's not important where we enter the cycle, only that we continue through all three, on and on in growing awareness and strategic action. Participants analyze the current social reality. From that analysis, actions are devised to resist the reality and to live alternatives. As actions are implemented, participants reflect on what is happening. And the cycle continues.

Circles seek a transforming shift in paradigm to Earth-size ways. We are not satisfied with incremental improvements that settle into nothing more than better MultiEarth ways. Participants are ever alert for actions and moments that are transformative.

Participants likely travel many spiritual paths so the spirituality of a Jubilee Circle can be rich. The core acknowledgement is simply that OneEarth living—living in the community of all Earth's elements and species—inherently involves the experiences of wonder, awe, amazement, and all else that is named by the word "spirit." Love, awe, and wonder of the heart are valued along with ideas and thoughts of the mind as we seek to effectively counter the structures of MultiEarth ways that weigh so heavily on the world. Public rituals that subvert MultiEarth's domination can be strengthened by including spirituality.

In a nutshell: Jubilee Circles form to enact what is in this Handbook and create what this Handbook has not yet thought of.

What Do Circles in the U.S. and Mexico Do?

All of these activities are ongoing, though no single Circle does all of them.

Circles Empower Women

- Over 30 women continue to develop their skill in art; many turn it into income.
- A 2017 workshop on the topic of micro-entrepreneurship was highly appreciated.
- Scores of women continue to be trained in their legal rights.
- Training and empowerment networks are being established to stop domestic and gender-based violence (in Mexico, one in three women is a victim of violence).
- Five women trained in the San Mateo Jubilee Circle now also teach other

women about art, crafts, care of the earth, and economies of solidarity.

Circles Tutor and Teach

- Scores of children receive tutoring every week throughout the school year.
- A guitarist gives weekly music lessons.
- Classes in theology and humanities are given in multiple congregations throughout southern Mexico.
- Over 40 persons are being trained in organic gardening by a horticulturalist.
- Each year we lead one or more delegations of people from the U.S. and Mexico to experience firsthand the practices of OneEarth Jubilee and resistance to MultiEarth powers in other communities and cultures.
- An organic garden provides some vegetables for three families and is a teaching lab for many more.

- Over 20 children, 2 to 4 years old, are trained in "early education" throughout the school year to explore their skills and skills with their moms and dads as a team.
- More than 70 children were in a one-week summer camp, learning more about the care of the land, visiting the organic garden, and working with recycling materials.
- A container of PET material is used by people in the community to recycle and reuse in crafts and art.
- A team of 15 young people works permanently for water care, through training, conferences and workshops, reforestation and sanitation of the natural basins of the hill of their community.
- The Cultural Center Daniel Swanson hosts 150 visitors a week in different classes, workshops, conferences, reading circles, meetings, etc.

Circles Deliver Medical Services and Healthcare

- A physician in the San Mateo Jubilee Circle delivers medical care and medicines to low-income households; she currently sees up to 20 people each week.
- Each year multiple workshops teach participants how to make non-commercial healthcare and cleaning products.
- Cooking classes for healthy eating are offered intermittently through the year with many eager participants.

Circles Create Blogs, Books, Circle Reports, and Podcasts

- Each month a new podcast is produced with 200+ in the audience.
- Three books have been published in 2017; one on forming Jubilee Circles.
- 2-3 new blogs are posted to the website each month.

- The website, www.casajubileo.org is continually updated.
- Each of the 3 Jubilee Circles makes 3-4 reports per year on their prolific activities; these reports are usually posted to the website.

Circles Use Money Frugally, Effectively

- We seek relationships with funders through 3 annual funding letters.
- We redistribute money and power from where there is more to where there is less. This is a theme we practice in all Circles. Each month the San Diego Circle redistributes money from donations received.

Circles Also...

- Produce 4 newsletters, *Jubileo,* annually and send them to over 400 subscribers.

- Have established partnerships on a couple of campuses, and hope for more.
- Collaborate with other organizations and Indigenous groups to continually increase the effectiveness of their Circle.
- Encourage one another's spiritual practices.

The Circle you form may well add to this list!

What Are People Saying About Circles?

From the Jubilee Circle in San Cristobal, Chiapas, MX: It is safe to say that we in Chiapas are very grateful to be in the family of jubilee.... We continue to learn from the other Circles how to continue building another world!

From a Person who benefitted from the Jubilee Circle in San Diego, California, US:

Thank you so much, San Diego Circle! I'm very grateful for all the connections you've made for me in Mexico. Will see how it goes but I'm excited! I hope I can also be of value to them. I'd like to get together with you when I return.

From the Jubilee Circle in San Mateo, Puebla, MX: I would like to interact more with the San Cristobal team. Tell us about your work there, give us feed back, and also encourage us to innovate using some ideas from your work there. Let´s continue working for a better world!

And again… Grace was a wonderful blessing for us, and specially for me. Yesterday we had a round table with entrepreneur women (mujeres emprendedoras). She shared about her experience in The Philippines and in other countries. The result of that is that we are going to continue meeting every week and see how we can start business together, including Artesanas Shalom. We are excited about dreams and visions. They were talking about creating a savings bank. So we will see....

How Can I Use This Handbook Effectively?

You can use this handbook personally to move further into OneEarth living. But you will be most effective if you use it in a small group, i.e., a Jubilee Circle. You will not be effective unless you recognize that MultiEarth and OneEarth are two entirely different paradigms. We must choose one or the other as the direction we want for our lives and society. When we consciously choose OneEarth ways, even if we as yet do not fully live them, we have set ourselves on course to live interdependent with all beings on our planet.

Contents

Choice

Themes

Actions

Appendix

1

Choice

[We are] privileged to live in a time when everything is at stake... and when our efforts make a difference in the eternal contest between the forces of togetherness and division, between justice and exploitation.

—"Granny D" of New Hampshire
speaking on her 93rd birthday

Choosing: OneEarth Jubilee or MultiEarth Ways

In Jubilee Circles our purpose is OneEarth living because we must live within the capacities of our one planet—the home we share with millions of other species.

We resist MultiEarth living because it exceeds our planet's capacities. MultiEarth living expresses the aspirations to accumulate wealth and power in our world. It results in lifestyles and systems that live beyond the means of our planet.

In sharp contrast, Jubilee Circles commit to share fully and democratically Earth's abundance. We believe that the most important strategy of resistance to MultiEarth ways is to empower alternatives that fully express OneEarth living. To achieve this transforming combination of resistance and alternatives, we invoke the historic strategy of Jubilee.

Jubilee is an expression of OneEarth living that speaks eloquently to our multiple crises in civilization and ecology. However, few know the story of how Jubilee has been invoked across centuries as an Earth-centered, creation-based strategy. Jubilee is a time-tested model of thought and action able to resist the exploitation of the planet and undo the oppression under which MultiEarth powers and empires place people and species. Jubilee goes beyond resisting injustices. It empowers intentions to live just and right relationships with Earth and all her inhabitants.

By invoking the OneEarth Jubilee amid the crises of our time, we stand in the tradition of those who have done so through many dark times.

Jubilee in the Earth Story and in the Civilization Story

There are two world-shaping stories underway on our planet. One tells about civilizing

Earth to fit human demands; the other tells of adapting to Earth's story. One tells how human egos arrange the world from their self-appointed position at the apex of nature's evolutionary story. The other tells how a more spiritual human, truer to nature's evolutionary intent for us, seeks to live interdependently with all species in Earth's community of life. Jubilee resists the former, but thrives in the latter.

We hear most about the story of human civilization with human's at the apex shaping the world as egos do it. This story so occupies what we call "news" that the second large story seems only for specialists who study it. Yet, the Earth eco-story is the older and more dynamic of the two stories and is the larger context in which the civilization story happens. Earth's story is shaped by dynamics far greater than what human egos can control. In her story, humans are not the apex, but integral to the dynamic interdependent, interrelated processes of life. We partly understand those processes. The rest fill us with wonder. Even so, for the majority of us, Earth's story is a secondary story—like a specialty shop for the few, rather than a supermarket for the many.

Or so it was!

Today the Earth story is getting in our faces. It's not just the meteorologists telling us about extreme weather. Nor the scientists telling us about new stars. Now, insurance companies are determining limits on which of the increasing natural disasters they will cover and for how much. The U.S. military is planning responses to increasing conflicts arising from migrations caused by job loss when regional mineral and oil resources are exhausted, or when land that has been farmed for centuries turns to desert, or when low lands and shorelines become submerged by rising waters.

Earth is speaking with increasing volume and frequency. Many of us hear her now; yet, many remain deaf. Or hearing, we rush to secure our privileges, power, and assets, not yet believing that Earth's story holds the remaining trump cards. To use a baseball metaphor, Earth bats last.

After reading this handbook on OneEarth Jubilee, be alert to which of these two stories is being talked about in the "news." We've been shaped to think that the story of human history is the only one, or at least the only one that really matters. But such ego-centrism contains within it the seeds of its own destruction. Those seeds have sprouted and are bearing some bad fruit. But turn to the OneEarth story, rooted in the truth of the Cosmos, and we can live bearing good fruit.

Where I grew up, in the rural Midwest—the years were 1940-1960—one farmer sometimes asked another, "Are you making any money?" A frequent answer was, "No, just making a living." That memory from my boyhood illustrates this handbook's contrast of paradigms: one is focused on making money, the other on making a living. If you want to make money, pick a model other than Jubilee, but expect dissonance with our planet and possible destruction by her. If you want to make a living, Jubilee serves well because it is amazingly integrated with our planet.

People, businesses, and governments commonly seek advantage, power, and control. The framework of Jubilee seeks to prevent domination, empire, and control, so it goes against what they are looking for.

In the world of Jubilee:

- All are invited to participate without partiality.

- All share in the resources of Earth, and do so with ecological reverence.
- Power is shared and passed around.
- Redistribution of resources and wealth move downward and outward instead of upward and to the center of power.
- Jubilee replaces hierarchies of power and wealth accumulation with equity.

Jubilee is typically absent from the histories of governments and corporations. But sort through the people's stories and histories and we find it being practiced in radically in-spirited ways.

What we need is a new Bottom Line, one which judges the various aspects of society by the qualities they cultivate in us... we [should] expect our society to promote love... compassion, kindness and generosity,... ethical and ecological sensitivity... [and we should] expect our society to nurture our capacity to respond to others as embodiments of the sacred and to the universe with gratitude, wonder and awe.

—Rabbi Michael Lerner

Examples of Invoking Jubilee Across History

We stand with the Jews and those of biblical times who invoked Jubilee to resist empires of the Mediterranean world.

We stand with the people of 18th century England who invoked Jubilee to resist the aristocracy's takeover of the common land.

We stand with the African slaves and the abolitionists in the U.S. who invoked Jubilee to end slavery.

We stand with democracy, symbolized by the Liberty Bell, on which is inscribed the Jubilee text of Leviticus 25:10.

We stand with today's Jubilee USA Network invoking Jubilee to forgive onerous debt of nations, student debt, and to reform international finance structures that perpetually benefit richer countries over poorer ones.

And, as the next two segments show, standing for Jubilee brings together Indigenous and non-Indigenous peoples; it commits us to just relationships with Earth herself and all her species.

Many Indigenous Peoples of the World Live Jubilee by Other Names

When a group of us went to the highlands of Mexico's southernmost state, Chiapas, during Holy Week, 2000, some of us spent

Holy Thursday night in Tzajalchen, a remote mountain community of a few hundred Indigenous people (Mayans) who had lost family and friends in a Dec. 23, 1997, massacre by a paramilitary group. That day 45 women, children, and men perished in the nearby community of Acteal. The elders of Tzajalchen told us how they had heard the gunfire on the mountainsides across the valley. Hours later their worst fears were confirmed. Their hearts were torn open. It deepened their resolve to practice assertive nonviolence. They named themselves Las Abejas (The Bees). Like bees in a highly functioning community around their queen, they reasoned, they were living around their Divine Queen.

They told us why NAFTA (North American Free Trade Agreement) was yet another form of genocide. How so? Because when NAFTA was negotiated, the Mexican constitution was changed so that the communal lands on which Indigenous peoples had always lived could be privately owned. But because the Mayans did not have the financial means to buy the land, the land gradually came under outside control. The Dominant System of foreign, corporate wealth and power was removing them from their ancestral land with all of its wealth of timber, oil, and uranium. They wanted us to hear how global corporations, with the full complicity of the Mexican and U.S. governments, treated them as "backward" and as an obstacle to "modernization." They explained how this "modernity" was destroying the eco-system, something they were obliged to protect by Divine commission. Later, one of the elders read a charge to us, commissioning us to be a voice for them, since, as Indians, they were voiceless in the Dominant Culture, especially in the North.

Our delegation had our eyes opened to see that as Indigenous people, past and present, lived "traditional ways," they were living what we were aspiring to by committing ourselves to Jubilee. I recalled the professors I'd had who said that Jubilee was mostly a quaint ideal—too utopian to have ever been truly practiced. I realized that my teachers had been blinded by the Dominant Culture's ways of thinking. In fact, Indigenous people have been living versions of Jubilee since the advent of our *Homo sapiens* ancestors.

Earth Is Crying Out for Jubilee in Today's Weather Extremes

I remember seeing my mother cry sometimes when her five kids and the schedule of the day simply overwhelmed her. Today, we've overwhelmed Mother Earth. And she's crying.

If you've seen summertime maps of the U.S. showing over half the states sweltering with endless days of 100 degree weather, soils and plants parched from little or no rain, then you've seen a map of MultiEarth, corporate-driven economics. You've also seen Earth crying for the ecological sanity of Jubilee lifestyles and practices.

On a July day in 2016, *Commondreams* posted such a map along with a quote from Drought Monitor author Richard Heim of the NOAA (Nat'l Oceanic and Atmospheric Administration):

> Temperatures reached 100 degrees Fahrenheit or hotter across parts of the Great Plains to the Midwest every day this week, and some locations have not had significant rain for the last 30 days. July 22, (2016), USDA statistics indicated over 90 percent of the topsoil was short or very short of moisture in Oklahoma, Kansas, Nebraska, Missouri, Iowa, Illinois, Indiana, and Ohio, with virtually all (99 percent) short or very short in Missouri and Illinois. Over 80 percent of the pasture and rangeland was in poor or very poor condition in Kansas, Arkansas, Missouri,

> Illinois, and Indiana. Corn, soybean, sorghum, and alfalfa losses continued to mount, ponds dried up, and wells failed in several of the states.

The Mother of all Earth's living is overwhelmed. Instead of complaining about how hot or how dry it is, we can stop ourselves, change attitudes, and turn our hearts to hear Mother Earth crying for our love. We can give her priority over whatever choices and conveniences we're putting ahead of her.

2

Themes

Just how challenging it is to live the OneEarth Jubilee becomes real for us when we devote ourselves to embodying it in our lives and societies. Each of the thirteen themes that follow will grow us into greater awareness of Earth-size ways. If put into practice, they will reshape our lives to fit our planet.

13 Jubilee Themes to Practice in Jubilee Circles

1. RESIST! Jubilee is part of what can well be called the Great Resistance that arose as a struggle against concentrations of power and wealth. In the Mediterranean region, where Western civilization was born, the Great Resistance stood against many aspects of the Neolithic Revolution (8,000 to 2000 B.C.E.). Over the centuries, Jubilee has resisted concentrations of resources and power that have been structured systematically to deprive some and privilege others. Today, transnational corporations, governments, and militaries form formidable systems of power. Transnationals generate legislation and policies that favor them, lobby governments to pass their compositions into law, and expect the militaries of nation-states to defend their interests. Jubilee resists such

practices and the thinking that justifies them.

2. **LAND** is sacred. No human can truly make it a private possession. In the language of spiritual thinking, land belongs to God. In the language of the marketplace, thinking of land as sacred means that it cannot justly be bought and sold as real estate or a financial asset without more negative than positive results. Land is commonwealth. Only what can be produced on land can be owned. Land itself is priceless and too powerful for human systems to manage justly. All efforts to own land in MultiEarth economic systems contribute to disparity and concentrations of power. Turning it into private wealth undermines Earth's community of life which Jubilee defends. Jubilee also works for the health of land. That's why eating organic food is so important. When land is used organically it sequesters carbon from the atmosphere. The soil gets richer; the air

gets cleaner; the climate becomes more stable; our food is healthier.

3. **COMMUNITY,** the interconnectedness of all things, is core to Jubilee. Earth's great commons and commonwealth assure that all can live with enough when sharing and cooperation are integral to the story by which we live. Deep in our souls we know that we are stronger through cooperation, more whole through sharing. Jubilee calls out these greater capacities of our humanness, capacities that are constantly compromised by our ego's insecurities which put "I" first. But our truer self is pained by ego's smallness, its desire for private mastery, and its craving for individual dominance. Jubilee Circles call forth our ego-transcending capacities. We then become intentional about living interdependently with all beings, not just with other humans. Maintaining ecological balance becomes far more important than a personal balance sheet. Larger

homes can be shared by more than one household. Intentional networks in a neighborhood can increase common meals and gardens. Preservation of species moves from an important option to being essential.

All life is interrelated, and we are all caught in an inescapable network of mutuality, tied in a single garment of destiny.

—Martin Luther King Jr.

4. **COMMONWEALTH** and the commons are closely linked with community. Jubilee protects and promotes commonwealth as our primary wealth. Wherever resources serve the common good, Jubilee Circles act to protect them from strategies by which they can become privately owned. Jubilee seeks alternatives to private ownership and public or government ownership. So, for example, community land trusts can help provide

basic housing for all by means of a legal vehicle that empowers a community to manage the land.

5. **DEMOCRACY** with the fullest possible participation is the Jubilee way in so far as it is also nature's way. Governing our lives together proceeds apace with the tempo and interdependence of the eco-region in which we live. Democracy inevitable slows things down in our expedited, fast track MultiEarth pace. We are required to listen, to value the speech from the hearts of others, to adjust, and increase our awareness around every decision being made.
6. **REDISTRIBUTION** outward from centers of accumulation and downward from hierarchies of power assures the continuation of Jubilee ways. The redistribution upward that happens continually in growth economics and MultiEarth civilization is reversed in OneEarth Jubilee. Decentralization and redistributive justice are built into

the calendar around holidays, into the decision-making of communities, and into spiritual practices of individuals and faith-based groups. These assure that we practice redistribution and increase our understanding of the intricacies and power of redistribution as we do so.

7. **DEBT** can serve only short term ends. Perhaps seven years, but no more. Debt develops disparity and separation—a hierarchy of more and less. Such hierarchy destroys not only human community and democracy, but the community and democracy embodied in Earth's total community of life. The interdependence of Earth's community is a sacred power on which life depends. Hence, long-term debt (beyond seven years) destroys life. Though debt is an essential mechanism in growth economies, it is systematically restricted in Jubilee.
8. **ENOUGH** brings a sense of sufficiency and abundance to lives lived in the

consciousness of Jubilee. By contrast, *enough* finds no meaningful use in a growth economy. Only *more* matters. The stress, anxiety, and scarcity thinking that go with chasing *more* is a constant in MultiEarth living. In Jubilee, when we accumulate more than *enough* it spoils. But this counters what MultiEarth ways teach. Learning to trust Earth's ways to provide all that life needs is a radical challenge to MultiEarth thought. Yet, a deeper trust of Earth as wild and sovereign, not just Earth as tamed and cultivated into monocultures, is interlocked with *enough* as a guiding element in Jubilee Circles and the OneEarth societies we shape.

9. **CRIME** is defined by those who rule. MultiEarth civilization criminalizes according to what violates the laws and arrangements that serve its ends. But OneEarth practices criminalize only what destroys the full community of life. In MultiEarth criminalization, felony

convictions not only imprison but commonly handicap a person far beyond the sentence they serve. By contrast, OneEarth ways restore offenders to community through practices of confession, forgiveness, reconciliation, and accountability. So in the Bible, Third Isaiah and Jesus speak of freeing the prisoner. Convictions based on the standards of criminalization imposed by MultiEarth civilization must be overturned and the convicts freed whenever the standards of conviction are not consistent with maintaining full participation in Earth's interrelated community of life.

10. NONVIOLENCE results from Jubilee's practices of cooperating and sharing with all of life instead of competing for more than what others have. Consequently, the need for enforcement via militaries and police falls off dramatically. Loving our neighbors, including all species, becomes an act of resistance to the powers and a way of life with strong returns.

11. **SPIRITUALITY** infuses all the elements of Jubilee. Without the Spirit of the Divine, the spirit of the age or the spirit of wealth will shape ego-driven lives. Following greater consciousness than what ego can muster is key to Jubilee. Consequently, seeing the world through many avenues—reason, observation, poetic imagination, dreams, music, dance, meditation—all are necessary for the awakening of consciousness that Jubilee living evokes from us. Jubilee recognizes the Presence (the sacred, Divine, God, Allah, YHWH, and other names used by various religious traditions) in nature and cosmos. Spirituality is inherent in the mystery and drama of the continuous, evolutionary unfolding of everything. However, MultiEarth's domination forecloses many experiences of the Spirit.
12. **REST** is integral to the rhythm of living Jubilee. When we watch creation, we observe its cycles of rest and activity. In

civilization's 24-7 pattern, rest is a subversive act. MultiEarth ways are ever in a hurry. Land is not rested. Workers must put in long hours to succeed. Food producing animals—cows, beef, hogs, and chickens—are confined, mechanized, and hurried to maximum productivity in the shortest time possible. Jubilee's rhythm breaks the hurry up pattern. It insists that we rest, reconnect with the worth of our own being, and invest time in interrelating.

13. **MACRO-STORIES** of Earth and Cosmos give to Jubilee a far older and bigger context than civilization's context which began only ten or twelve thousand years ago. Consequently, OneEarth Jubilee uses different standards of measure—for example, wellbeing of Earth and all life rather than profits or success. Jubilee, by other names, has antecedents with our early ancestors. The mystery and size of its continuing story guide us in a way that rational and strategic

planning alone cannot. Its vision stirs human imagination to shape the better OneEarth world that is possible.

3

Actions

20 Actions for Jubilee Circles

Jubilee Circles reshape life and society from supersize to Earth-size. They help us fit our lives INSIDE our planet's full community of life—all 20 million+ species. Trained as we are to live in MultiEarth, super-size ways, in Circles we continue to retrain ourselves in OneEarth, Earth-size ways. Some of the following actions are especially for U.S. citizens. Jubilee Circles in other nations will want to adapt actions that fit their contexts.

Without pretending to be a complete list, these 20 actions illustrate the transformative retraining that happens through Jubilee Circles. Your Circle may add to this list.

Allies interested in retraining are essential.

1. Find allies—Find people and organizations to link up with on ecological and civilizational crises. Individual actions fall short of what is now needed. We need a mobilization of the size and speed that happened when the U.S. entered WWII.

Policies are major retraining tools and influence a major effort.

2. Citizen's lobbying—Let policy makers know that we care a whole lot, not just a little bit, about climate change, soils and waters, air and species. Work with *Citizens Climate Lobby* (https://citizensclimatelobby.org/). Exercise influence

in groups, various media, workplaces, and governing bodies, ever encouraging OneEarth choices.

3. Citizen's public actions—Show in public demonstrations that we want to get to OneEarth living as fast as possible—by 2050 if not before.
4. Voting—Make ecological crises a primary criterion on who we vote for and let candidates know our intention. Check this state-by-state guide for voting environmentally for some big help (http://www.streetdirectory.com/travel_guide/2671/family/an_environmental_voting_guide_for_us_state_elections.html).
5. Influence—Bring as many retraining ideas and actions as possible to the organizations we are in. The Free Management Library has suggestions to help (http://managementhelp.org/leadingpeople/influencing-others.htm).

Food choices and systems move us to OneEarth living even more than energy choices.

6. Organics—Eating organically grown food in our home is an action with great impact. We are wise to be as vigorous about it as possible. Organic growing actually takes carbon out of the air whereas non-organic growing puts carbon into the air. The Rodale Institute has a great report on this (https://rodaleinstitute.org/reversing-climate-change-achievable-by-farming-organically/); Yale has another (http://e360.yale.edu/features/soil_as_carbon_storehouse_new_weapon_in_climate_fight).
7. Eating out—We can choose restaurants that serve locally sourced, organic foods. By avoiding large chain restaurants and fast-food chains we resist participating in operations that do not operate with a consciousness for Earth-size living. The supply chain from farm to plate (or

fast food container) of most such eating places does not follow OneEarth practices in the treatment of animals, health, land use, local waterways, air quality, or food waste. Websites in your area are likely available as guides for choosing such restaurants. Eat Well has a guide (http://www.eatwellguide.org/guides); so does Local Harvest (https://www.localharvest.org/restaurants/).

8. Eating a low-meat diet—Producing enough meat for high-meat eating diets treats animals poorly, adds methane gas to the air, and contributes to deforesting for grazing. By moving to low-meat diets we have great impact for healthy eco-regions. Shrink That Footprint compares five diets (http://shrinkthatfootprint.com/food-carbon-footprint-diet) to conclude low-meat diets help us live much more sustainably on our planet. The Environment Journal weighs in with confirming arguments

(http://shrinkthatfootprint.com/food-carbon-footprint-diet).

9. Grow some food—Whether we grow food in a large garden, farm, or a patio container, growing food performs the miracle of reconnecting us to dirt and all the things plants teach us when we work with them. Plants retrain us toward OneEarth living, increasing well-being for us and the planet.

Finance management for our households—also for organizations and workplaces when we have influence in those settings.

10. Bank locally—Any of us with accounts in a mega-bank are supporting MultiEarth ways. It's important that we move our money to a locally owned bank, a credit union, or a community development bank—institutions where our money is far more likely to align with our decision to move toward OneEarth living. The American Independent Business

Alliance gives important reasons (https://www.amiba.net/resources/why-bank-independent/) and research for making this decision. The Institute for Local Self-Reliance gives us their five arguments (https://ilsr.org/top-5-reasons-choose-community-bank-or-credit-union/).

11. Invest and divest–If we have a portfolio of investments, we want to remember that money talks, so we want it to speak the language of OneEarth living. We will want to work with an Independent Registered Financial Advisor (not a brokerage firm), and be sure they spend time seeking out funds and projects committed to the ecological and civilizational goals we have. For example, if we are currently invested in any carbon fuel operations, we can divest and go to all clean energies. Most likely, it will strengthen our portfolio to do so. Green America provides reliable guidance in

this tricky area of investing and divesting (https://www.greenamerica.org/socially-responsible-investing). Choosing a truly helpful financial advisor is another important piece. So read here (https://www.naturalinvestments.com/advisors/loving/) and here (https://www.arcadvisers.net/resources/) for two examples of things to look for. One of the biggest challenges Jubilee makes to investment portfolios and inheritance plans is to think in terms of *enough* rather than *more*.

12. Credit cards—Credit cards are a lucrative business for banks. Because the majority of credit cards are offered through major banks, they serve MultiEarth structures. Banks collect multiple fees: annual fees, interest fees, and a fee with every transaction. We can choose credit cards that tilt more toward OneEarth living (https://www.greenamerica.org/responsible-credit-cards).

Local economies resist globalization—a process led by transnational institutions and cooperating governments that is a wholly MultiEarth effort.

Jubilee wants to keep money in the local economy; large corporations remove money from the local economy. The more money circulates within a locale, the more the economy there is strengthened.

13. Imports—We can eliminate many imports from our lives. Localization is the best antidote to globalization. It also eliminates the pollution to which transportation contributes. Many international trade experts agree (http://www.tradeready.ca/2016/trade-takeaways/face-off-buy-local-vs-buy-global/).
14. Locally-owned businesses—We can resist buying from chains and online behemoths like Amazon as much as possible. Whenever we purchase from a locally owned business, our money circulates

longer in our local community where it strengthens our community's economy, stability, and stewardship. Business Alliance for Local Living Economies, BALLE (https://bealocalist.org/), is a leader in the field of building local economies (http://www.yesmagazine.org/commonomics/welcome-to-commonomics-how-to-build-local-economies-strong-enough-for-everyone) as is Neighborhood Economics (http://neighborhoodeconomics.org/ecosystem-vs-egosystem/). Using a local bank (https://ilsr.org/top-5-reasons-choose-community-bank-or-credit-union/) and avoiding big banks is a most important choice.

The impacts of our transportation and travel can be reduced by changing some of our habits.

Jubilee seeks out the most ecological transportation. Combinations of walking, bicycling, and public transit are the first choice rather than automatically getting into a car.

15. Walking—When we go less than a mile, walking is a great choice. We get exercise we need, notice more of what's in that mile, put no emissions into the air—there are easily 10 or more reasons (http://www.huffingtonpost.com/amy-arndt/walking-transportation_b_4559012.html) for us to increase walking as a means of transportation.
16. Bicycles and public transit—Buses, trolleys, and trains let us read, have down time, use our phones or laptops, and get us out of the bubble of our cars and traffic. It's definitely not a waste of time and greatly reduces emissions. As with walking, there's easily ten, a dozen, or more reasons to bike for transportation (https://www.mnn.com/green-tech/transportation/stories/12-reasons-to-start-using-a-bicycle-

for-transportation) and to use public transit (https://www.treehugger.com/htgg/how-to-go-green-public-transportation.html).

17. Greener trips—Buses are greenest, including express buses such as Megabus that connect some cities. Next come hybrid cars, trains, and coach jets. Worst? SUVs and first-class jets produce more than 1 pound of CO_2 per mile. Regular cars are in the middle. For local trips, use an electric car if you can afford one. Pooling rides is a habit to be developed. By the way, all cruises are highly polluting. *The Union of Concerned Scientists underscores the importance of greening our travel* (http://www.ucsusa.org/clean-vehicles).

Psycho-spiritual work is essential in our retraining for OneEarth living.

Relocating ourselves from outside eco-spheres to inside, and from the consciousness of egos to the consciousness of our greater Self, is the psycho-spiritual part of retraining. Actions #18-20 take us on the psycho-spiritual path, as explained more fully in my book, *From Egos to Eden: Our Heroic Journey to Keep Earth Livable* (http://theoneearthproject.com/from-egos-to-eden-1/). Some online sources also speak to this path, though many are timid about this part of the journey.

18. Partner with nature's powers—Relocate ourselves from enjoying and controlling nature as outsiders to being insiders. Let her humanize us as we picture ourselves with the other species as partners inside Earth's total community of all life. We leave behind the sense of privilege toward other species that comes with MultiEarth thinking.
19. Evolve to new humans—MultiEarth living happens in ego consciousness. Retraining for OneEarth living requires a shift in our psyches (souls). We must struggle with our egos so that our core

identity is no longer centered in our egos but in our greater souls. This process of dethroning the ego and enthroning a greater Self is a psycho-spiritual struggle of heroic proportion, a metamorphosis to being a new human. Only spiritual paths that pursue this change can get us to OneEarth living.

20. Live in Spiritual Consciousness—New humans retrain to live in the topography of Spiritual Consciousness, the consciousness essential to OneEarth living. Consciousness controlled by egos becomes deeply unsatisfying in Spiritual Consciousness because we become attracted to the deeper energies that are trans-rational and trans-personal.

4 Actions to Take After You've Read This Minibook

1. Form a Jubilee Circle. Start fresh, or revise a group you are already in. If you want coaching, contact us—619-528-8075 or lee@jubilee-economics.org.
2. Get ideas from the reports of other Jubilee Circles at www.casajubileo.org. Click on the tab entitled "Circle Reports."
3. Begin planning for your future weeklong pilgrimage to Jubilee Circles in Mexico. Click on the tab entitled "Delegations" at www.casajubileo.org.
4. Once your Jubilee Circle is underway, use all your social media to share with others what your Jubilee Circle is doing.

"Never doubt that a small group of thoughtful, committed citizens can change the world; indeed, it's the only thing that ever has."

—Margaret Mead (1901-1978),
cultural anthropologist

Imagination and Art in Retraining Ourselves

It is our inner artist who will help us re-image, re-shape our worlds into the abundance economics required in the [coming] Ecozoic Era. The rational powers, so essential over the past several centuries, though still important, must now share the task with the powers of image-ination. —Lewis Hyde,

The Gift: Imagination and the Erotic Life Property

4

Appendix

Connecting Jubilee Circles with Jubilee in the Bible

Some Circles may not be inclined to use the Bible, so it's important to be clear that Jubilee Circles do not require a biblical connection. Other Circles may regard the Bible as adding strength to their understanding and practice of OneEarth Jubilee. Either way works.

Where the Jubilee Name Comes From

By now it is apparent that Jubilee is so much more than a 50th anniversary. Jubilee provides dynamic resistance to what's harming Earth and life and spells out alternatives for our communities and our planet. When we put the contents of Jubilee into action we generate the better world that we are capable of.

The name "Jubilee" comes from an obscure part of the Bible—Leviticus 25, part of Judaism's Torah. But its significance for ecology, economics, and spirituality spreads across the Bible and beyond. Leviticus 25 describes a 50th year in which the "Happy New Year" celebration begins on Yom Kippur, or the Day of Atonement, in the Jewish calendar. To mark Yom Kippur is to make an appointment with atonement, put it in our calendars, and give persistent attention to setting things right. Or, as the 12 Steps of AA tell us, to make amends for the wrongs we've committed in whatever way others have been affected by them. As originally envisioned, Jubilee was to be a year-long focus on repairing damage done. Jubilee gives particular attention to making right the wrongs connected to land, property, and property rights. And because it is also a seventh or sabbath year, debts are forgiven and slaves set free.

The etymology of "Jubilee" is not entirely certain, but *yobel* is the Hebrew word translated as "Jubilee" in Leviticus. Because Yom Kippur opened by blowing blasts on a ram's horn (shofar) throughout the land, the Greeks, in their translation of the Jewish Bible, translated the word *yobel* as "a trumpet blast of liberty." Later still, when the Bible was translated into Latin (Vulgate translation), the translators further emphasized the act of blasting and exulting by translating *yobel* with the word *jubilo,* meaning "shout". So "Jubilee" is an exultation that arises as we feel liberated from the failures and oppressions that have been holding us back. Given that Jubilee involved correcting wrongs that happened through transactions of land, property, property rights, debts, and slavery, it needed to be a year long—time enough to unravel the wrongs and correct them. It was a year to bring things back to where everyone had a share again—a kind of reunion or homebringing.

To say that Jubilee, as a name for a particular shape of OneEarth living, comes from the Torah or Bible, while true, fails to reveal the exhilarating emotions and energies that happen when festering injustices are corrected! When we're wronged regarding where we live, our health, our ability to learn, freedom to express ourselves thoughtfully, our spiritual practice, our workplace, or our rights, we feel it personally. So when the wrong is corrected, we feel the liberation. Spontaneous eruptions of our hearts, blasting on trumpets (shofars), and shouting *(jubilo)* joyfully would be part of a year dedicated to correcting these wrongs. Jubilee, then, comes from the heart—the heart that excitedly shouts out and shares its experience of new life as injustice is corrected.

Jubilee in the Bible

Uses of the Bible among people with nationalist, anti-science views and politically right agendas abound. Jubilee counters those in every way while providing guidance for forward-thinking, OneEarth living.

Jubilee in the Biblical Conflict between Empire (MultiEarth) and Creation (OneEarth)—Look again at how the Bible speaks to the economics that generates justice and injustice, wealth and poverty, power and marginalization. Note that the Bible's overarching story opposes empires and their way of arranging economies to favor power, to concentrate wealth, and thereby to construct social and economic hierarchies. The writings in the Bible present the tension between empire and creation, and take a position. Writings dissent from the economic and societal models used by a succession of empires in the Middle East, including Egypt, Assyria, Babylon, Persia, Greece, Rome, and others less at the core of the biblical narrative.

Extensive segments of the Bible describe Israel's own experience with empire in the era of their monarchs—David, Solomon, and successors. That experience evolved into a failed experiment.

Fast forward to Jesus and see how he not only spoke in vigorous opposition to the economic oppressions of Rome's imperial domination, he rejected popular appeals to live his life as a new David or Solomon. Instead, he lived a messianic consciousness that rejected the empire model. He taught this consciousness as essential to living in God's "kingdom." This conversion of consciousness gave people a far greater capacity to share and cooperate—both essentials in living the model he called the "kingdom of God." That "kingdom" emphasized the commons more than privatized land, commonwealth more than private assets, and living in the abundance of Creation's limits more than seeking empire's advantages or successes. This "kingdom" took the Jubilee economy that was part of his Jewish heritage and reinvented it. It was a startling alternative to Rome's domination and empire economics.

Correcting Jubilee's Underplayed Presence in the Bible—For most people in faith-based organizations—from congregations to campuses to nonprofits—Jubilee's presence in the Bible is underplayed, if mentioned at all. However, Jubilee is making a comeback. Some biblical scholarship of the past couple of decades is rediscovering Jubilee, revealing a stronger presence of Jubilee than previously recognized. Blindness to seeing Jubilee in biblical writings has come in part because the Bible continues to be seen through the lenses of growth economics and capitalism.

In the past, the understanding has been that Jubilee is explicitly invoked or practiced in only limited passages.—The following list provides a set of starter references to Jubilee in the Bible.

- From the Torah (the first five books of the Old Testament)
  - Exodus 16, 21:2-6, 23:10-11
  - Leviticus 25
  - Deuteronomy 15:1-18
- From the Old Testament History of Empires
  - Nehemiah 5:1-13
- From the Old Testament Prophets
  - Isaiah 58, 61:1-2
  - Jeremiah 34:8-22
- From the Gospels, Acts, and Epistles in the New Testament
  - Matthew 5:3-10, 6:9-13
  - Luke 4:16-30
  - Acts 2:43-47, 4:32-37
  - II Corinthians 8:10-14

When Jubilee is perceived in only these passages, the common conclusion is that Jubilee was an ideal too utopian to ever be sustained. It was invoked only in a few moments of protest or renewal, all of which soon faded away. Such a conclusion reinforces the thinking among most people professing biblical faith that Jubilee is impractical, obscure, and quaint, but doesn't merit attention as a viable practice for today. To break out of such a dismissal of this biblical alternative, consider the three points that follow.

1. **Jubilee is not a one-shot experiment that was given up on.**—It is noteworthy that the above biblical passages come from many different authors over centuries of time and report on a millennium of history—a millennium during which the people of the Bible experienced "empire religion" by way of the imperial succession of Egypt, Babylon, Assyria, Greece, and Rome. Jubilee was part of an alternative and larger worldview. Some people committed to resisting empire did so by practicing as much of Jubilee as they could. It helped give them strength amid imperial injustices and renewal of Spirit where souls were going dry.

2. **Jubilee is part of the Bible's preferred worldview that makes Creation the context and measure of all life, from economics to religion.**—When placed in a larger worldview, these explicit references to Jubilee become part of an expansive way of thinking, living, and shaping society. With advances in biblical studies in recent decades, many are concluding that Jubilee was and is a viable alternative. Wes Howard-Brook, at the University of Seattle and author of *Come Out, My People: God's Call Out of Empire in the Bible and Beyond* (Orbis, 2010), sees the Bible as a compilation of two major worldviews: (1) empire religion and (2) creation religion. These parallel the MultiEarth and OneEarth worldviews used elsewhere in this handbook. The Jubilee passages listed above all advance the economic-ecological attitude, actions, and worldview of "creation religion." The only

exception is the Nehemiah passage in which Jubilee is used by imperial rule as a temporary strategy to resolve a dispute between people whose privileges differed. Following exile in Babylon, land ownership during the years of reconstruction in Judea and Jerusalem was governed by Nehemiah and Ezra who were under the direction of Persia's empire (Iran on today's map). Peasants on the land were shortchanged in the process. When they cried out against their plight to Nehemiah, he invoked Jubilee for some respite for them, but not as an ongoing way of life.

3. **Jubilee is most accurately understood from the perspective of oppressed people.** The Jubilee passages in the Bible come from the perspective of a people oppressed by empire and the dominant culture's way of thinking. Looking in from the margins of empire and feeling with the heart of the oppressed helps

> us read Jubilee and the Bible with different eyes. From this vantage point, we see how the people in the Bible strayed from Jubilee because the policies, enforcements, and seductions of empire religion, along with the imperial domination of society, were often too alluring or coercive to resist. Reading the Torah, the Prophets, and Jesus from the perspective of the margins, we hear them urging people to trust the practicality of Jubilee along with the trustworthiness of YHWH, the God who urges that it be guidance for true life.

Today, Jubilee calls us to resist the reigning contemporary empires and superpowers expressed through Wall Street, the U.S. with its expansive militarism, the globalized economy, and the world's richest and most powerful countries. Most especially Jubilee calls us to resist injustices that the imperial worldview perpetrates. Our resistance focuses less on what's wrong with the imperial way than on the positive actions of living Jubilee as the more just, creation-based alternative.

But if we don't read the Bible with eyes to see Jubilee as integral to the creation-based worldview, then we miss its larger and most compelling significance, namely its guidance for designing our businesses, congregations, campuses, and households according to it.

Brief Comments on Foundational Jubilee Texts in the Bible

Jubilee expresses a worldview in which the biblical Jubilee year is a core element. Jubilee societies are scaled to fit our one planet home. The structures of Jubilee give all humans and creatures access to Creation's abundance, an abundance within the limits of Earth's capacities and distributed democratically so that all have enough.

Jubilee contrasts with state controlled, corporate controlled, or any centrally controlled economy and society, be they bent toward socialism, capitalism, or some other vision. These texts variously imagine or prescribe Jubilee as an alternative to the common practices of the culture that prevailed at the time.

- **Leviticus 25** is the Jubilee year passage. It prohibits the private ownership of land. Crops are "owned" but the land belongs to YHWH.
- **Deuteronomy 15** is an important seventh year or sabbath year debt cancellation/ forgiveness statement.
- **Exodus 16** is an important seventh day or sabbath day story in which each day enough is provided from the abundance of nature in order to sustain life. But any who sought to accumulate more found that the "more" would rot. This story is later cited by Jesus in John 6 following the special feeding story of a multitude and by Paul in II Corinthians 8 when a "Jubilee sharing" is being encouraged between followers of the Way of Jesus in Corinth and those in Jerusalem.
- **Nehemiah 5** shows Jubilee being used by Nehemiah to settle a dispute during

Judea's reconstruction under Persia's imperial rule. Cyrus, having defeated Babylon, simultaneously curried favor with Jews and also extended Persia's imperial reach into Judea by releasing the Jews from Babylon. They'd been brought there following Babylon's destruction of Jerusalem in 587 BCE. Those excited by Cyrus' proclamation of release, pulled up from Babylon where they'd been for decades. When they returned to Judea, too much time had elapsed for them to know anyone living there anymore. They were, nonetheless, returning to their homeland. But those who now resided in Judea did not take kindly to these "settlers" from Babylon. Nehemiah sought to settle the disputes between resident Judeans and new settlers by invoking Jubilee— at least temporarily. I say temporarily because Jubilee does not lend itself to longterm imperial expansion.

- **Isaiah 58 and 61:1-3** present a poetic, prophetic rendition of Jubilee. Instead of a Jubilee 50th year, Isaiah suggests living "an acceptable year of the Lord" every year. He uses the Jubilee model, itemizing some of its key themes in the poetry of Hebrew parallelism.

- **Jeremiah 34:8-22** focuses on freeing slaves. It reports how in the closing years of the monarchy of Judea, just before the destruction of Jerusalem and pillage of Judea by the empire of Babylon, King Zedekiah made an agreement with the people that they must free any slave who'd worked for them at least six years. The agreement was soon broken, reflecting on both the weak authority of the monarchy at the time and the fact that Jubilee does not fit a monarchy's ways of operating.
- **Luke 4:16-21**—When Luke presents Jesus in a "gospel," he is writing after Rome's empire destroyed Jerusalem and the Temple (70 CE). Luke opens the curtain on Jesus' public life in the synagogue of his hometown, Nazareth. There Jesus reads the Jubilee passage from Isaiah 61, but curiously includes a line also from

Isaiah 58, connecting those two passages quite explicitly. As his Gospel continues, Luke reveals the life and activities of Jesus as an incarnation of Jubilee. Jesus brings good news to the poor in contrast to the injustices brought by Rome's domination, the superpower of the day. He opens the eyes of the blind—sometimes the physical eyes with which we see, but far more often the inner eyes of illumination or consciousness by which we see the world differently. Opened eyes especially see empires differently and see through their claims to authority. He teaches his disciples to pray for a Jubilee in what we call the Lord's Prayer or "Our Father." That prayer immediately protests calling the Roman emperor "Father" by addressing God with the name instead. It hallows or makes sacred the divine name on Earth, discrediting the rulers (political and economic) who seek divine right and authority. It seeks daily bread instead of accumulated wealth. It urges forgiveness and cancellation of debt (moral and economic) instead of using debt to redistribute wealth from those with less to those with more. It appeals for the coming of the kingdom that embodied an economy of commonwealth for the common good instead of private wealth and vast inequalities.

- **Acts 2, 4,** and continuing—The Spirit comes upon people (echoing Isaiah 61 and Luke 4) and when she/it (Spirit is feminine in Hebrew; neuter in Greek; never masculine) does, people convert from the Spirit of the Age or the Spirit of the Times to the Spirit of YHWH. New behaviors include sharing of houses, teachings, daily bread, and holding things in common. Sharing/cooperation/community—what is richly embodied in the Greek word *koinonia*—is a 180 degree conversion from the habits of accumulation, competition, and privatization that are practiced in the societies of superpowers, empires, and corporate-controlled economies.

- **II Corinthians 8:10-14**—Paul urges the community of people in Corinth (c. 60 CE), who had been called out of empire, to practice what had been roundly embraced by those in Jerusalem's called-out community. He asks them to think in terms of abundance and to share with those in Jerusalem who at that moment were feeling need. Paul appeals to the Corinthian group to practice the Jubilee elements of abundance, redistribution, and enough.

All the species thank you for reading this Handbook... and enacting Jubilee!

Purchase Other OneEarth Publishing Books

- **Please** write reviews and "Customer Comments" wherever you can. All your comments let others know your thoughts and encourage increased readership of these books.

  From Egos to Eden: Our Heroic Journey to Keep Earth Livable, Lee Van Ham

  Blinded by Progress: Breaking Out of the Illusion that Holds Us, Lee Van Ham

  Light, Bright, Damn Near White, Richard Lawrence

  A Tree for Troubles, Cheryl Johnson

Contact us: 619-528-8075 email lee@jubilee-economics.org

Follow websites: www.casajubileo.org and www.theoneearthproject.com

Appreciation goes...

- to Linda McKee for underwriting most of the publishing costs;
- to readers of an early version who provided many helpful suggestions—Randall Mullins, Angelica Juarez Jimenez, Greg Newswanger, Paul Taylor, Gerald Iversen, Doug Clegg, Emo Yango, John Poole, Juanita Mangan-Van Ham;
- to David Wogahn for first suggesting the minibook size, for his counsel on design, and for handling the logistics of publication through his company, AuthorImprints.

Jubilee Circles: A Guide to OneEarth Living
Lee Van Ham (with Richard Lawrence)

Published by OneEarth Publishing
3295 Meade Ave., San Diego, CA 92116

http://www.theoneearthproject.com

Author contact information:
lee@jubilee-economics.org

Publishing Services: AuthorImprints.com